SMA
J2010
94/09/29
$17.95

2. UN
3. Armed Forces.
4. Refugees.

Sexsmith Secondary School Library

ORGANIZATIONS THAT HELP THE WORLD

UNITED NATIONS HIGH COMMISSIONER FOR REFUGEES

JEAN TRIER

OTHER TITLES IN THE SERIES
Amnesty International by Marsha Bronson (1-85015-307-8)
Greenpeace by Paul Brown (1-85015-366-3)
United Nations by Michael Pollard (1-85015-306-X)
The Red Cross and the Red Crescent by Michael Pollard (1-85015-305-1)
World Wide Fund for Nature by Peter Denton (1-85015-367-1)

Picture Credits:
AKG: 28/Berlin; **Amnesty International:** 30; **Gamma:** 4-5/Marc Deville, 6/Marlene Daniels, 7/Chip Hires, 8-9/Marc Deville, 10 (top)/Marc Deville, 10 (bottom)/Chip Hires, 11/Chip Hires, 12 (top)/K.Bernstein/ITN, 12 (bottom)/ITN/FSP, 13/Richards, 14/Marlene Daniels, 15 (right)/Noel Quidu, 18 (top)/Daher, 20 (top and bottom)/Turpin, 27/Alain Buu, 33/Turpin, 38/Aventurier, 40/Richard Tomkins, 41 (top)/Clavieres, 41 (bottom)/Vogel, 42/Patrick Bar, 45/Bonnecarrere, 46 (top left)/Liais, 46 (bottom right)/Roger Job, 50/Nevery, 52/K.Bernstein, 58/Wildenberg, 60/K.Bernstein; **The Guardian:** 15 (left)/Gary Weaser; **Rex Features:** 25 (top)/SIPA/Gentile, 25 (bottom)/Stills, 53; **Sygma:** 36-37/Pavlovsky; **UN:** 24 (top), 54-55/Müller; **UNHCR:** cover, 16 (top), 16 (bottom)/Sanders, 17, 19/A. Hollman, 21/Errington, 22 (top)/A.Hollman, 22 (bottom)/H. Eloaguen, 23/A.Hollman, 24 (bottom), 26/Brissaud, 29, 31, 34/Van de Linde, 39/Buzzouro, 43/A.Hollman, 46 (bottom left), 46-47/Girard, 47 (bottom), 48/Errington, 49 (top), 49 (bottom)/Taylor, 56/de Toledo, 59 (top)/S.Lahuzen, 59 (bottom)/A.Hollman; **UNO:** 18 (bottom).

Special thanks to UNHCR Photographic Library, Geneva and Mohammed Lounes, Gamma, Paris, for their help on picture research.

The story of Hamdija Suhonjic (pp.14-15) written by Edward Pilkington used by permission of and copyright © 1993 The Guardian.

Published in Great Britain in 1994
by Exley Publications Ltd,
16 Chalk Hill, Watford,
Herts WD1 4BN, United Kingdom.

Copyright © Exley Publications, 1994
Copyright © Jean Trier, 1994

A copy of the CIP data is available from the British Library on request.

ISBN 1-85015-365-5

All rights reserved. No part of this publication may be reproduced or transmitted in any form or by any means, electronic or mechanical, including photocopy, recording or any information storage and retrieval system without permission in writing from the Publisher.

Series editor: Helen Exley
Editor: Samantha Armstrong
Editorial Assistant: Helen Lanz
Picture editors: Alex Goldberg and James Clift of Image Select
Typeset by Delta Print, Watford, Herts, U.K.
Printed by Kultura, Budapest

UNITED NATIONS HIGH COMMISSIONER FOR REFUGEES

JEAN TRIER

Flee for your lives

"They're coming. The tanks and helicopters are coming!" The news spread like wildfire through the towns and villages. Artillery gunfire could be heard rumbling threateningly in the distance. Fear whipped everyone into action. The streets emptied. People frantically collected their belongings together – just a few bare essentials – some food and water, blankets, a cooking pot – and fled up into the mountains.

Thousands upon thousands of men, women and children struggled up the steep track. Most had to walk carrying their possessions on their backs or heads. Many held babies or small children in their arms. Some supported the old or the sick. A few had

Above: Having fled bombing from Saddam Hussein's Iraqi troops, 250,000 Kurds crossed into Turkey, 200,000 remained on the Iraq-Turkey border and a further 1.4 million people headed for the Iran-Iraq border.

Previous page: Kurds wait to cross from Iraq to Turkey. The Kurds, persecuted since the 1920s when their homeland was divided, fled as the countries around them clashed in warfare and some Kurds themselves fought for an independent homeland.

vehicles but many of these soon broke down or ran out of fuel. The track became littered with abandoned objects – trucks, piles of clothing, mattresses – things that the exhausted families could not carry a step further.

It was a perilous journey, on one side of the track the bare mountainside rose to snow-capped peaks and, on the other, was a steeply-plunging slope. There was no shelter from the icy mountain wind, the rain and the driving snow. There was nowhere to hide from the enemy who pursued them on the ground and from the air. They had to hurry. Those who could not keep up died beside the track. Their families could only stop long enough to bury them in the rocky earth. Food and water soon became desperately scarce; many people ran out completely and went for days without either.

Who were all these people, winding their way like a seemingly endless bright ribbon through the bleak mountains? They were Kurds who, in April 1991, fled from their homes in Iraq in fear of the forces of the Iraqi government after the Gulf War. They fled to the north, making for the borders of Iran and Turkey, hoping that these countries would take them in and give them asylum or a safe place to stay. They were refugees, people fleeing their country in fear of their lives.

The situation was incredible and unique. Two million people had fled almost overnight and were sleeping rough in the freezing mountains. The government of Iran did its best to help but was overwhelmed by the sheer scale of numbers. On the Turkish border – an almost imaginary line in the mountains – the situation was even worse. Here the Kurds' makeshift camps clung to the mountainside. Their "tents" were often just scraps of polythene slung between sparse trees. The only water came from melted snow, fetched from higher up by those who still had enough strength left to collect it. Hundreds of people were dying every day.

The world *had* to do something.

Taking control

The job of saving the Kurds fell to the world's largest organization protecting and working with refugees, the United Nations High Commissioner for Refugees (UNHCR).

Its headquarters in Geneva, Switzerland, were alive with activity. Even before the Gulf War began in 1990, the United Nations (UN) had prepared a plan of action to make sure that surrounding countries were ready to help with the refugees that were expected to result from the conflict. The UN had planned for one hundred thousand refugees, but now there were over two million.

It wasn't just a matter of taking care of their immediate food and shelter needs. There was no way that the two million refugees could be accommodated in Turkey or Iran for any length of time and, left where they were inside Iraq, the fleeing Kurds could be attacked and slaughtered by Iraqi forces at any moment.

The Gulf War allies, with the support of the UN, decided to establish a "safe haven" for the Kurds in

Following page: The rows of tents at the UNHCR transit camp at Silopi in Turkey was a welcome sight for the Kurdish people. Silopi was a forward staging post from which the Kurds could gradually return, along the "Blue Routes", to the "safe havens" set up by the UN.

In those forty-eight hours in April 1991, many Kurds left their homes without any warning or time to prepare for the treacherous journey through the mountains. The UNHCR was quick to respond to this, the fastest flow of refugees in its history.

northern Iraq that would be protected by allied troops. It was the first time that the UN had taken direct control of events in this way; inside the territory of an independent nation.

A lifeline for the Kurds

Meanwhile, in the special operations room of the UNHCR in Geneva, the necessities for survival were being organized as quickly as possible. The top priority was to get the refugees off the mountains.
  Telephones rang continuously as supplies of food,

Above: Food is distributed at Ishikveren, one of eight major Kurdish camps along the mountainous border between Iraq and Turkey. Huge quantities of food were airlifted in by the UNHCR but conditions were poor – no toilets, no power supply, very little water. All this, along with overcrowding, made diseases, such as dysentery, difficult to control. Medical aid was provided (right) to try to redress the balance.

tents and medical equipment were found and airlifted to the scene in conditions of appalling difficulty. The bad weather, which had caused the deaths of so many refugees, now hampered the rescuers, too.

"Blue Routes" home

Under pressure from the UN, the Iraqi government agreed to allow those refugees who wanted to, to return home.

A series of transit camps was set up between the mountains where the Kurds were, and the plains, where the Kurds lived. The camps were on specially-marked routes, known as "Blue Routes" after the blue of the UN flag. At each camp, returning refugees were given all the necessary assistance for their journey. Transport was provided too – convoys of vehicles, each with their UN flag – were soon ferrying thousands of refugees back down to the plains of Iraq.

This exodus of Kurds, and their subsequent return which began a mere six weeks later, were perhaps the fastest mass movements on such a scale in refugee history. Hundreds of UNHCR relief workers and thousands of UN troops were involved in the rescue and follow-up plans. When the refugees were finally returned to their homes – or what was left of them as the Iraqis had destroyed many of the villages – emergency aid had to be supplied as well. The UNHCR also continued to look after those refugees who chose to stay in Iran or Turkey because they were too scared to return to Iraq.

Remember the Kurds?

But, inevitably, the media interest in the Kurds was short-lived. The images of their suffering soon disappeared from television screens and newspapers around the world as new stories took over the headlines. People soon forgot the Kurds.

Within a year another disastrous calamity was creating yet more refugees – the civil war in former Yugoslavia. Firstly, in Croatia and then in Bosnia, as different ethnic and religious groups fought for

Shooting flames as high as a fifty-storey building, seven hundred of Kuwait's oil wells poured toxic smoke high into the sky, blocking out the sun. Set alight by the retreating forces of Saddam Hussein in the Gulf War in January 1991, it took nine months to put the fires out.

"Given the magnitude and complexity of the problem, it is easy to forget that refugees are first and foremost individual human beings, not an abstract problem."

Sadako Ogata, United Nations High Commissioner for Refugees, 1991.

Above and opposite: Starved, beaten or murdered, thousands of former Yugoslavs were victims of ethnic cleansing. Families of mixed religion were torn apart. Terror shows on the faces of this family in Sarajevo as the father leaves for a different country.

dominance. Villagers found themselves fighting and killing people that they had lived next to for years. It was a vicious war which was fought from village to village across the country.

Ethnic cleansing

This time a hideous new phrase entered the language: ethnic cleansing. People were killed, raped and forced from their villages at gun point simply because of their religious beliefs. Terrified families fled their homes in their numbers.

Again nearby countries were faced with an influx of refugees. Europe had not seen anything like it since World War II – over two million people were on the move, fleeing their houses, leaving *everything* they possessed, desperately trying to find a place where they would not be persecuted.

Once more, the columns of white trucks with the UNHCR emblem, stubbornly trying to get food and medical aid through to the starving people stuck in

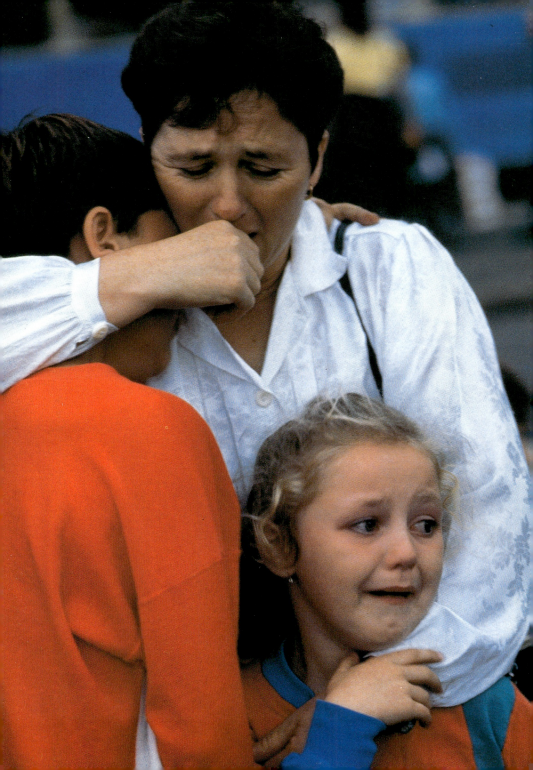

CASE HISTORY 1

The story of Hamdija Suhonjic

'Hamdija Suhonjic was in the bathroom shaving when the phone rang. It was his sister in Germany: "Brother, I have some bad news."
He was told of the deaths of his wife, Safija, and his daughter, Mirzeta. It was the news he had feared ever since he was brought to London [England] as one of the first groups of Bosnian Muslims to be rescued from Serbian concentration camps.
The last time he saw his wife and daughter was on Thursday morning, July 2, [1992].
At 5:20a.m. they were woken by banging on the front door. His neighbour, a Serbian, had come to ask him to attend the police station for a routine interview. "I didn't even say goodbye. Why should I? I would be back within the hour. I even put on my best suit," he says.
But out of the house he knew something was wrong. They drove in the opposite direction to the police station before going to the Keraterm camp.
He was lucky to survive the next two months. He almost suffocated while being taken in a small van to the Omarska camp. One night he saw men beaten to death. He had his nose broken with a baton. By the time he was rescued from a third camp, he was suffering from starvation and dysentery. On September 15 the International Committee of the Red Cross picked out Hamdija as [needing] urgent medical treatment. "I asked what would happen to my wife and daughters. They said ... our families would join us as soon as possible." But it took lawyers months to complete the cumbersome process of applying to the Home Office.

Behind the barbed wire in Sarajevo, the besieged capital of Bosnia. Food supplies to its people were frequently interrupted and the city was without fuel and electricity for days or even weeks on end.

the ransacked villages and bombed towns, appeared on television screens. The UNHCR, the conscience of the world, was again left with the problem of saving lives.

Beginnings

The idea of asylum, of providing a place of safety for those fleeing their homes and in fear for their lives, is not new. It is found throughout history. The right

His fears grew every day compounded by news of the ethnic cleansing.
At the beginning of April he was heartened by a phone call from Mirzeta. She was in a buoyant mood and they were looking forward to their new life in England. But on April 7 the Home Office announced that his wife would be allowed to come but daughters Azra and Mirzeta were ineligible. It is thought that Safija refused to leave her children behind.

Azra was lucky. She gained permission to live in Switzerland where her husband has relatives. Serbian thugs struck either on the night of Friday or Saturday, May 7 or 8. Hamdija suspects that his wife and daughter were raped before their throats were cut.

"I cannot change my skin for another person's, so I'll just have to live through it. Who knows, maybe I'll be able to laugh again one day." Hamdija has no photographs of his family. His only memento is a note that the Red Cross brought him. "I, mother, Azra and her family are all well and healthy," it says. "It's only that we are missing you. We love you lots. Mirzeta."
The Home Office said: "There are thousands like this in Bosnia. We cannot take everybody."

to seek sanctuary is one of civilization's oldest principles. From the Ancient Greeks to the Aztecs, through Judaism to Islam, people have welcomed the persecuted stranger and given them asylum.

They have done so, tragically, because refugee movements have always been a feature of human history. But it is only in the twentieth century that the world has begun to take united action to relieve the suffering of refugees. Even then, it took two world wars, which uprooted and scattered millions of

Above: Homes throughout the former Yugoslavia, like this one in Bosnia, were simply ripped apart by shelling in the civil war. Above left: Hamdija Suhonjic has found himself detached from his home, culture and country, and will never see his family again.

Above: The identity card introduced for refugees in Europe in 1922. The international community, through the League of Nations, acted together for the first time to protect and help those such as the despairing German woman below, forced from her home by conflict.

people, to finally produce an organization with responsibility for all the world's refugees.

In the spirit of Nansen

A start was made in 1921, when the newly-formed League of Nations appointed the Arctic explorer, Fridtjof Nansen, as its first High Commissioner for Refugees. Nansen had been working with the International Red Cross in Russia after the 1917 revolution, directing relief operations among the huge numbers of people who were starving there.

Nansen was a courageous and humanitarian figure, who made a striking impression in Geneva with his tall, angular body and white hair. He recognized that meticulous planning and attention to detail were essential if any impact was to be made on the huge refugee problem remaining after World War I. One of the key things he did was to introduce special identity cards, nicknamed "Nansen passports", for refugees who had no identification papers. These were recognized in fifty-two countries. In 1922, Nansen was awarded the Nobel Prize for Peace and he used the money for international relief work.

Fridtjof Nansen died in 1930 but the spirit of his organization continued to inspire the work of those caring for refugees. The growing number of refugees fleeing from the rise to power of Adolf Hitler's Nazis and World War II continued to put pressure on the world to do something.

The formation of the UNHCR

World War II ended with a chaotic refugee situation. Thirty million people had been uprooted from their homes and refugees were scattered all across the face of the world.

A huge, temporary rehabilitation scheme was initiated by the newly-formed United Nations and it returned or resettled most of the people. But it was obvious that, in the long term, the UN would have to take some kind of responsibility for people who continued to flee from persecution.

The UN set up a body that would, as far as possible, operate independently. The Office of the United Nations High Commissioner for Refugees (UNHCR) started work on January 1, 1951 and was given a mandate to operate for three years. It was to work independently but with all the authority and prestige of a non-political UN organization. This would enable it to work with governments to ensure fair treatment and international protection for all refugees.

A problem that nobody wants

The UNHCR started with just thirty-three staff, most of them lawyers and secretaries. They faced a daunting task because of one central underlying problem – the fact that refugees, everywhere, are unpopular. Nobody wants them.

The country from which they are fleeing rarely has any sympathy for them, they may have been an unwanted and persecuted ethnic group, they may

In the first half of the twentieth century there were huge movements of refugees in Europe brought about by conflicts such as the Balkan Wars, the Russian Revolution and the two World Wars. In its early years, the UNHCR was mainly called upon to help refugees in Europe. These refugees were usually resettled in another European country. They then became part of the community and citizens of the host country and could lead normal, self-sufficient lives.

have been critical of their country or they may be associated with people engaged in armed revolt against injustice in their country. They are fugitives and their government is anxious that as little attention as possible is given to their graphic stories of torture, beating or lack of freedom. As far as the government is concerned the refugees should just disappear, as silently as possible.

When the refugees first cross the borders into new countries and details of atrocities are revealed, there is, at first, a huge wave of public sympathy for their plight. But when this trickle of refugees becomes a flood, and there are hundreds of thousands or millions of people involved, the barriers go up.

The first place that the people flee to, the host country or the country of first asylum, is inundated; its emergency and relief services cannot cope and its people see scarce resources being given to the newcomers, or asylum seekers. Within weeks the initial sympathy wears thin.

Then comes the most difficult question of all – which countries are going to give permanent homes to those asylum seekers? If there are large numbers of people involved, who is going to face the political wrath of inviting these numbers of new immigrants into their society?

These are the fundamental questions that lie at the heart of every solution to every refugee problem. They are the problems that the staff of the UNHCR try to solve every day they go to work.

Protection – the first task

Fleeing, whether from Bosnia (above top) or from the oppressive government in Burma (above), the right to seek asylum is ancient. The shame is that it is still needed and increasingly so with refugee populations in nearly every country.

In its mandate, the UNHCR was given two basic tasks. Firstly, to provide international protection for refugees and secondly, to find long term solutions to their problems. It also had an emergency role, to keep refugees alive while searching for these long-term solutions.

As soon as people flee from their country, the UNHCR takes on its first responsibility to protect them. As well as food, water and shelter, they need the protection of the law – both internationally and within the country where they have taken refuge.

They must not be forced to return unwillingly to the country from which they have just fled.

Two basic international laws protect them, the 1951 UN Convention relating to the status of refugees and the 1967 Protocol. These give a definition of who can be officially recognized as a refugee and outlines how they should be treated.

Having ensured the immediate survival of the asylum seekers, the UNHCR has to try and ensure that they continue to be well treated in that country of first asylum and decide who legally qualifies as a "refugee".

Who is a refugee?

Before the UNHCR can begin its second task of finding long-term solutions, it must establish that the asylum seekers are refugees according to the 1951 UN Convention.

This Convention gives a very specific definition of a refugee as someone who has fled across an international border because of a "well-founded fear

"A refugee is above all a victim...a person who, 'owing to well-founded fear of persecution for reasons of race, religion, nationality, membership of a particular social group or political opinion, is outside the country of his nationality and is unable, or unwilling to avail himself of the protection of that country...'."

From the 1951 Convention and the 1967 Protocol relating to the status of refugees.

Asylum seekers have their papers checked in Hungary. The UNHCR has to decide on their status quickly and fairly.

Case History 2

Nineteen years of turmoil and civil war

"Aideed was a senior government official in Ethiopia until 1974, when Emperor Haile Selassie was overthrown. As a member of the overthrown government, Aideed was arrested and tortured with electric shocks...his arms and legs were broken and all his teeth knocked out. In 1977, during a rebel attack, Aideed managed to escape. He collected his wife and children and walked day and night until they reached Sudan. They spent the next eleven years in a refugee camp.

"I worked in the camp as a volunteer.... I also pushed my children to do the same because I was hoping that if, one day, we returned to our country they should be able to contribute to rebuilding it."

Then, civil war broke out in Sudan and Aideed and his family fled again – to the south of the country. Here Aideed's wife became ill and died. "The years since her death have been the worst in my life," Aideed says. "I still tried to go on for the sake of the children but I prayed every day to be helped or to die." The war reached the south of the country and Aideed and his children had to flee again, this time to Kenya. He is still there helping others in another refugee camp. "There are hundreds of people here who have been injured, tortured and raped. I thought that as I cannot help all the 25,000 refugees in this camp, the least I can do it is try to support some of the wounded and the disabled...."

of persecution". This means that they must have left their own country and have done so against their will. Persecution might be physical violence, a threat to life or harassment and wrongful arrest. It can take many forms – political, religious or racial.

In recent years, however, this "official" definition of a refugee has tended to raise almost as many questions as it answers.

In 1984 during a famine in Ethiopia, for instance, there were many different people who were all starving. Local people were not considered refugees because they lived there. There were people starving who *had* been refugees when they fled to nearby Somalia, but were no longer refugees because they had returned to Ethiopia. There were people who had fled from other parts of Ethiopia to escape fighting by rival political forces, but were not refugees because they had only fled from one part of the country to another and had not crossed any international borders. Finally, there were "genuine" refugees, people who had fled from fighting in

> *"We are not over-populated; we are under-organized, under-funded and under-educated."*
>
> An Ethiopian relief official, from "Africa in Crisis".

Opposite and below: In Sudan, Somalia and Ethiopia there were over 2,000,000 people who fled civil war. Fighting in these areas, combined with drought, contributed to the famines of the 1970s and 1980s.

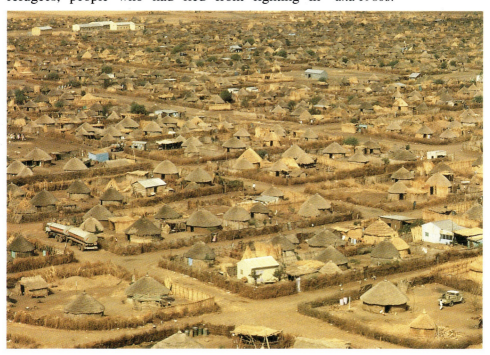

The long process of seeking asylum begins at the border where travel documents are checked. While cases are heard, individuals wait in transit camps for months, even years.

Somalia. All four groups were starving in the same area but only those from Somalia were refugees according to international law. In a case like this it would be inhuman – and impossible – for the UNHCR to help only the Somalis without helping the other people who were in just as much need.

Impossible situation

A similar situation occurred when the two million Kurdish refugees camped in the mountains of northern Iraq, Turkey and Iran.

It would have been impossible to determine who among them was in individual fear of persecution. The UNHCR simply had to act and stretch the legal definition of "refugees" to save lives.

The UNHCR also faces a further problem in trying to define "who is a refugee?" because of the existence of "economic migrants". In previous decades, many people had little idea how wealthy other parts of the world really were. Now television reaches even remote areas and desperate people can see the wealth of other countries.

If they have the remotest chance they vote against poverty with their feet, illegally crossing international borders in search of jobs and prosperity. If they are caught they can be arrested for illegal entry. Some of these migrants then claim persecution and refugee status; they are called "economic migrants" because they have left for financial reasons.

Somewhere to go

Once it has been decided that the asylum seekers are refugees who qualify for the UNHCR's protection, the UNHCR can begin to look for a long-term solution to the problems of the refugees.

There are three usual solutions. The first and best is "repatriation". This means the refugees return home voluntarily to their country of origin as soon as it is safe to do so. Once there, the UNHCR helps the "returnees", as they are called, move back in to the community. This is particularly necessary if they

have been away for a long time or if there has been a great deal of devastation in the home country.

The second is "integration into the country of first asylum". The last solution is "resettlement" in another country altogether. This is generally the UNHCR's least preferred solution as it means involving a third country and is often most unsettling and costly for all concerned.

Closed doors

The biggest problem of all facing refugees is that, so often, every door is slammed shut in their faces.

People all over the world are sympathetic to the plight of refugees; they are horrified when they see the suffering that has caused a group of people to flee and willingly contribute money and urge their governments to "do something".

But the governments of the wealthier nations of North America, Europe, Asia and Australasia have

With little else to do, an asylum seeker rests his head in his arms at reception rooms at Geneva airport, in Switzerland. In some countries asylum requests may take months to process. As the number of asylum seekers – and economic migrants – in Europe increases, so too does the backlog of unheard cases. Some governments respond by tightening entry controls. Some of the methods used have aroused the UNHCR's concern.

Above: The Protocol to the 1951 UN Convention relating to the status of refugees was approved on January 31, 1967, in New York.
Below: The UNHCR emblem.

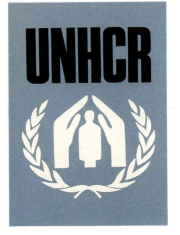

increasingly tried to limit immigration, whether of economic migrant or persecuted refugees. This poses a huge problem for the UNHCR.

To try to achieve an "open door" policy, the UNHCR works directly with governments on behalf of refugees. It encourages countries to become signatories to the 1951 UN Refugee Convention so that they accept the UN definition of a refugee and the international standards on how asylum seekers and refugees should be treated. By the end of 1993, over 120 states – about two-thirds of the countries in the world – had signed the Convention.

The UNHCR then takes responsibility for making sure that these countries meet the required standards of the UN Convention, especially in ensuring that no one is forcibly sent back to their home country if they would be in danger there.

The UNHCR also encourages countries to have liberal asylum policies. This means allowing asylum seekers to enter different countries easily. On arrival in a country, asylum seekers have to go through legal procedures, often carried out by immigration and

Case History 3

Ana Romero, sixteen – in danger because her family knew too much

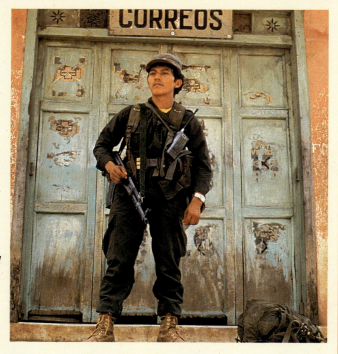

"My kindergarten in El Salvador was near a cemetery. Every morning on the way to school, I would see bodies piled up there, waiting for their graves. There was a lot of killing and torture going on. People got killed just for complaining about all the injustice in El Salvador.

"My dad was a photojournalist. He would go to places where people had been killed and take

pictures of them, so that their families would have a way to identify them. One day, my father was told he was in great danger. So we got out of El Salvador as fast as we could, without passports or money." The family fled to Los Angeles, USA illegally, the children were not sent to school for a long time because the parents were terrified they would be discovered and sent back to probable death in El Salvador. Six years later, the United States gave them permission to stay.

"I'm happy," says Ana. But I miss El Salvador...."

The population in El Salvador is five million, twenty thousand of that number are refugees from elsewhere. Many Salvadoreans themselves fled to other countries, including the United States, during the 1980s to escape the civil war and death squads linked to the tyrannical regime in power there.

Mrs. Sadako Ogata was elected High Commissioner for Refugees by the United Nations in 1991. During her first three-year post, she initiated a "Year of Repatriation" in 1992 and visited refugee situations, seeing for herself what needed to be done. She was re-elected for a further five years in 1993.

Opposite: The Chinese New Year is a cause for great celebration among the Chinese people. But, during the disputes between Vietnam and China in the 1970s and 1980s, Chinese people in Vietnam were persecuted for acts of worship.

border officials, and the UNHCR sees that these are carried out with as little delay as possible. Decisions on refugee status and a permanent solution can then be made swiftly.

The UNHCR also negotiates with governments to encourage them to provide places for those refugees who are in urgent need of resettlement. It tries to find the best resettlement opportunities for both able-bodied refugees and refugees with any physical disabilities and gets special schemes organized to help them all when they arrive. But, before the UNHCR can start a special scheme, it has to be asked to do so by the host country – the UNHCR can only succeed with the close cooperation of each country.

Headquarters

At the UNHCR's headquarters in Geneva the team faces a huge task. By the early 1990s, there were approximately nineteen million refugees in the world and the UNHCR's staff numbered around 3,000. About a quarter of the staff, who come from many different parts of the world, are based in Geneva. This office is the central point of the UNHCR's operations. Using the latest technology, refugee situations are monitored closely and international assistance is carefully coordinated.

In a major international emergency, the amount of organization that needs to be done from Geneva can be daunting. The headquarters staff have to find – and move – vast amounts of food, clothing, tents, trucks and medical equipment by air and by sea and start making deliveries within hours, rather than days, if they are to save lives.

A network of over one hundred offices radiates out from Geneva to over eighty countries. Regional offices supply essential data to Geneva. Officers within the different regions, called Representatives, give support to individual refugees and ensure that refugees are treated according to the rules of international protection. In the field, staff carry out the detailed work of emergency relief.

UNHCR staff have to be flexible; they can find themselves working in almost any part of the world,

CASE HISTORY 4

Mrs. Sang Guek Tang: forbidden to follow her religion

'Mrs. Tang comes from Cambodia. She is ethnically Chinese and, in 1975, was forced by the Khmer Rouge to live near the Thai border.

"The Khmer Rouge men persecuted me very badly because I could not see at night due to malnutrition so I was unable to work at night. They said to me they were going to kill all Chinese." In 1979, the Khmer Rouge regime was removed by invading Vietnamese troops – but the persecution of ethnic Chinese continued. They were not allowed to celebrate religious events, and Mrs. Tang was caught celebrating the Chinese New Year.

"I was taken to the police headquarters; a large amount of my money was confiscated and I was told that, if I celebrated my religion again, they would confiscate my property ... and I would be imprisoned.

My mother was then killed in the prison in May 1985 because she asked for her house back from the government.

In December 1985, my husband was shot dead by the police because he was accused of selling rice to the Khmer Rouge...when the police came to our house he tried to escape by bicycle but was shot and died on the road."

Mrs. Tang tried to sell rice in the local market but was bullied by the local government officer. "He repeatedly threatened to confiscate my rice and demanded money. He also intimidated me and raped me twice in 1990 at my home. He also reported me to the government and I was repeatedly persecuted and raped."

Mrs. Tang fled and, with the help of friends, got to Australia. On arrival, she was confined to a refugee camp for several more years, pleading all the time to the UNHCR to find her a country that would give her refuge. "We have all suffered enough for the last twenty years and we are still suffering. What we are asking now is to let us live in peace and freedom. Please help us...."'

with a great deal of upheaval and sacrifice in their personal and family lives. They can be away from home for years at a time and the work can be dangerous because helping refugees is sometimes seen as taking sides by the combatants in a war or civil war.

All kinds of help

The UNHCR is the largest organization concerned solely with refugees – but its task would be impossible without the help of many other different agencies. It works with UN agencies, such as the World Health Organization (WHO).

It also works, in the field, with voluntary non-governmental organizations. These have specialized skills and in-depth knowledge of each situation and are often involved in all the stages of a UNHCR operation. They put its plans into practice.

They help with the basic relief in emergency situations as well as giving advice, organizing education and training schemes and health care, and the setting up of income-generating projects for the refugees to earn money. They also help with the running of general community life.

The early years

When the UNHCR began its work in 1951 there were about one million refugees around the world. Several hundred thousand of these were in refugee camps in Europe, the last unsettled people from the thirty million or so uprooted by World War II.

Six years after the end of the war, they were still in "temporary" camps and no long-term solution to their plight had been found. Many of them did not want to go back to their country of origin because their suffering there had been so great. They hoped for a better life elsewhere.

Eventually, by patient work with governments, the UNHCR arranged resettlement. Many of the refugees were placed in countries on the other side of the world, particularly in Australia.

But even as the refugees from World War II were

A Soviet soldier lies dead in a Budapest street. After much devastation and bloodshed in fierce street-fighting, in which unarmed Hungarian rebels took on the might of Soviet tanks, the 1956 uprising in Hungary finally collapsed. Thousands of Hungarians then fled across the borders to Austria and Yugoslavia. This was one of the first large refugee outflows with which the UNHCR dealt.

being resettled, new flows of refugees began in Europe. These were mainly brought about by the denial of human rights in the new communist regimes in Eastern Europe. Anyone who showed the slightest opposition to the government in those countries faced harassment or arrest by police and other state agencies. There was a lot of wrongful imprisonment. Many people tried to escape to the West. In all, over five million people fled from Poland, Czechoslovakia, Hungary and the Soviet Union between 1945 and 1970.

Gathering speed

The number of refugees from the Eastern bloc countries suddenly swelled. In 1956, a major uprising in Hungary was swiftly and forcefully crushed by a Soviet invasion. Refugees poured out of Hungary, moving mainly at night, led by highly-paid guides. Soviet troops tried to close the borders but terrified Hungarians continued to stream out, risking

Despite the rather gloomy appearance of this barrack-like building in Austria, it was still a refuge for thousands of people, such as those leaving Hungary in 1956. It was not "home" for long as the UNHCR found long-term solutions to the refugee problem quickly at that time. Some 200,000 refugees from Hungary were resettled within two years.

Case History 5

Masood: tortured

'Masood is twenty-eight and was involved in trying to bring democracy to Afghanistan.

"Six years ago, my sister was arrested. I never heard of her again. Five years ago, my parents and brothers were arrested. I never heard of them again either. Then, one night when I left the bakery where I was working, I was arrested and thrown into a car by people dressed in ordinary civilian clothes.

"I tried to escape but was shot in the leg. I was bleeding heavily but, instead of being taken to hospital, I was brought to prison, blindfolded. I was beaten with fists, then with a special weapon with a rubber handle and a metal ball at the end. My nose, face and body were seriously injured. When I started to lose consciousness I was thrown in the 'cable room' with my hands tied behind my back. The torturers then beat me with electrical wires on the soles of my feet."

The next day, to avoid further torture, Masood pretended to cooperate in providing information.

"When the guards realized this, they took me to another room, tied me to a cross and poured petrol over me. I was left there for

many hours to decide whether or not I would talk, under the threat of being burned alive."

In an incredible cat-and-mouse game, Masood was then hospitalized by the torturers because his kidneys had been so badly beaten that they stopped working.

"I was given dialysis several times a day. As my legs were broken in several places they had to insert steel rods to hold the bones together. As soon as I was slightly better, I was taken back to prison and the torture continued. I was beaten and burned with cigarettes."

Once again the beatings took him to the edge of death and he was once again restored to hospital by his torturers. "Then I understood. They did not want me to die; they wanted me to stay alive and be mentally and physically destroyed." While he was in hospital for the second time, a male nurse bravely drugged the guards with sleeping pills and left with Masood for the border, where he escaped and got help from the UNHCR.

Masood broke into tears many times in giving this interview, and was truamatized by his experiences for years afterwards. He eventually found sanctuary as a refugee in Denmark.'

minefields and heavily-armed border guards. Some two hundred thousand refugees fled in all, mainly to Austria and Yugoslavia. Most of them were resettled within two years.

International Refugee Year

UNHCR work such as this helped to inspire the International Refugee Year in 1959. This drew public attention to the problems and needs of refugees throughout the world and funds were raised in a variety of ways. For example, seventy-five countries donated money from the sale of special stamps.

The money was used to help integrate refugees into their country of asylum and many of the refugee camps in Europe were finally closed as permanent houses were built for the refugees. Countries that had previously not been involved in the international effort to care for refugees now offered resettlement places for them. All this widened horizons and opened up possibilities for the resettlement of refugees in the future.

A Palestinian Arab boy stands outside his "home", the mud-hut refugee camp Ein Es Sultan in Jordan. About eight thousand children live in the camp and make up about half its population. The camp is the responsibility of a special agency set up to give assistance, such as food, medical and education services, to the tens of thousands of Palestinians who became refugees when Israel was created in 1948. Some Palestinians have been refugees for over forty years. If a peace process begun in 1993 succeeds, this boy may one day have a homeland.

But, in 1959, there was no way of knowing that the refugee situations were not winding down, they were growing. Every year, it seemed, the steady exodus of homeless people grew.

Still a temporary organization

In 1961, for example, the government of Macao asked the UNHCR for help with 120,000 refugees from mainland China who had flooded into this tiny country of only six square miles [9.6 km^2]. Macao had taken in a steady flow of refugees from China for several years, but this flood was equal to half of its total population. The refugees were crammed into shanty towns that were bursting at the seams. How could they possibly cope?

By the end of the UNHCR's first decade there were two million refugees in the world and, by that time, the UNHCR's original three year mandate had already been renewed twice. It has been renewed every five years ever since and the UNHCR is still seen, officially, as a temporary organization that will no longer be needed when the problem of the world's refugees has been solved.

Meanwhile, the number of refugees has climbed every year.

Africa sets the pace

The UNHCR also gained experience in dealing with floods of refugees when the colonial empires around the world ended. After World War II, colonies – countries ruled from a distance by another country – claimed their independence as rapidly as possible. But the transition from colonial rule to independence was not without trauma, particularly in Africa. Civil wars often created minority groups that had no choice but flight from persecution.

One of the first such mass exoduses in Africa occurred as a result of war in Algeria. Some two hundred thousand refugees sought asylum in Morocco and Tunisia where they had to live in conditions of terrible poverty and deprivation. In 1957, the UNHCR intervened on behalf of the

"Refugees are the people who run away from their places when there is fighting. There is no food. There is no freedom. There is no peace. That is what makes people run away from their places and they become refugees."

George, aged thirteen, a refugee from Uganda.

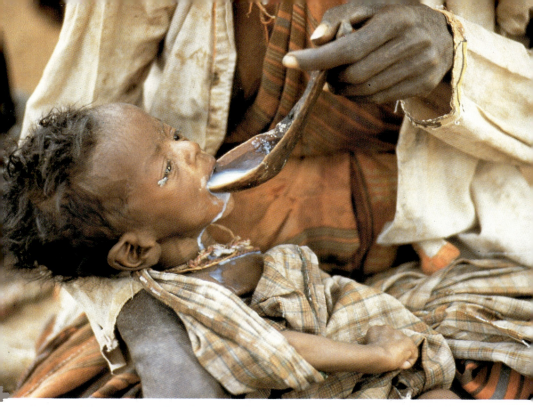

refugees. The war continued for eight years until Algeria finally achieved independence from France in 1963. Then the UNHCR was, at last, able to assist the refugees to return home.

In 1966, the UNHCR airlifted three thousand people from the terrible bloodshed in war-torn Congo to the safety of Tanzania. In the same year, the UNHCR helped thousands of refugees from a war of independence in Mozambique. After overseeing their welfare for ten years, the UNHCR then assisted them all to return home once the war was over. Meanwhile, in the north of Africa, hundreds of thousands of refugees fled from civil war in the Sudan. After eight years of exile and under the protection of the UNHCR, the Sudanese refugees were able to return home and were helped to resettle by the UNHCR.

But the UNHCR was again urgently needed in Tanzania when over 150,000 refugees fled there from the war in Burundi. Working with the government, the

A malnourished child receives its ration of food at an aid unit in Somalia. Africa has the largest concentration of refugees in the world. In times of drought, when survival is naturally difficult but possible, wars tip the balance causing severe famines that bring mass starvation in their wake. The UNHCR and other humanitarian agencies must supply immediate aid – but a long-term solution is most needed.

Unloading an airlift of supplies to southern Sudan in Africa where the UNHCR assisted refugees and displaced people during a civil war that has taken place, on and off, for over thirty-five years. This was one of the UNHCR's earliest attempts to deal with mass movements of people and provide huge quantities of supplies. It proved valuable experience for use in later crises around the world and introduced the UNHCR to many of the special problems of Africa.

UNHCR organized agricultural settlements for them.

The UNHCR was successfully involved in all the refugee crises that blew up in Africa during the 1960s and 1970s. It gained a great deal of experience that helped to develop the organizational skills at which it has come to excel. But the scale of refugee problems was still growing.

Stretched to the limit

In 1972 the UNHCR dealt with its first emergency involving *millions* of people.

In April and May of that year, some ten million Bengalis suddenly fled from a bitter and bloody civil war in East Pakistan across the border into India. In a matter of weeks, seven million people had arrived in India and the flow continued at the rate of fifty thousand more each day.

The refugees presented a tragic spectacle of human misery as they arrived and tried to find shelter in makeshift camps. "They don't even have straw huts," said a doctor in one camp, "and it is doubtful whether we could control an outbreak of cholera." At first, food was desperately short. People waited hours for a small portion of rice and half a cup of milk for the children – if they were lucky.

The exodus represented one of the most serious refugee problems that century. Cholera raged out of control in the hot months of June and the Indian government closed the border to stop the flow of refugees. The huge humanitarian crisis was finally solved with the creation of the new state of Bangladesh after India's 1971 war with Pakistan. The Bengalis were then able to return to their own country.

Planning in advance

Sometimes, with advance planning, it is possible to anticipate the worst effects of a refugee exodus. In 1971, for instance, the Ugandan military dictator, Idi Amin, suddenly ordered the expulsion of tens of thousands of people of Asian origin from Uganda. Many had been there for years with several generations of their families but they did not have Ugandan passports and were told to leave.

Idi Amin let his troops run riot and the Asian people fled in terror as army trucks roared down the streets where they waited for passports; families were robbed of their last money and possessions. In this case, the UNHCR, operating on pre-arranged plans, organized planes for immediate evacuation and set up transit camps for the refugees. Because of advance planning, the UNHCR was also able to arrange resettlement in twenty-five countries in Europe and North America that had already agreed to take the refugees.

Until the mid-1970s, the system set up in 1951 generally worked fairly well. But then came a massive explosion in the problem of the world's refugees that brought new and even greater challenges to the UNHCR. One of these explosions was the Vietnamese "boat people".

"Peace is more than just absence of war. It is rather a state in which no people of any country, in fact no group of people of any kind, live in fear or in need."

G.J. van Heuven Goedhart, High Commissioner for Refugees, 1954.

The problem of the boat people

In 1975, tens of thousands of people began to flee from Vietnam, Cambodia and Laos. They were desperately trying to escape from the killing fields of Cambodia and from Saigon after its fall at the end of the Vietnam War. More than a million people were murdered by the Communist guerrilla forces, the Khmer Rouge, so whole families trekked on foot to Thailand and China and embarked on boats to Hong Kong, Malaysia and the Philippines.

The stories of the perilous voyages of the "boat people", as they became known, across the South China Sea became famous worldwide.

A typical voyage might start with a huddled group

Happy to arrive, these Vietnamese have risked their lives in this tiny, overloaded, wooden boat. Their name, "boat people", was a measure of their desperation to leave the oppression and poverty of Vietnam.

Previous page: Just some of the Vietnamese men, women and children, desperately trying to leave their country on whatever transport they could find.

of people waiting near an isolated beach for a wind that would blow them out to sea, and, they hoped, to safety.

Dozens of families, hundreds of people in all, would cram together on the deck of a small, rickety fishing boat. Having to sit still – there was no room to move about – they would sleep where they sat.

In the open sea, the small boat would rock and shake, leaving the families seasick and exhausted so that they could hardly eat any of the sparse food. But they were always thirsty and the drinking water often ran out. Children and the elderly suffered the most – some would die. Help sometimes came from passing fishermen who would exchange water and food for a few possessions.

Sailing throughout the night, the boat people were always dependent on the weather. If the wind dropped, the boat would simply stop. An attack by pirates, who would murder or abduct them, was a real fear. If they were becalmed, bobbing helplessly up and down like a cork, they were a sitting target in the open sea. In the dark it must have been terrifying.

The shortage of drinking water, and food, was a constant problem. The small boats would rely on the help of passing ships but often these would ignore them, not wanting the trouble of taking hundreds of illegal immigrants on board. Sometimes, when luck was on the side of the fleeing refugees, local fishermen would take pity on them and tow the overburdened boats to safety.

Survivors

On the boats that did make it to their main destination, Hong Kong, the passengers were in for more shocks. Officials boarded their boat and, after several hours, they were allowed ashore. The refugees were taken to join the thousands of others who had made the same perilous voyage and were now living, crowded together, in huge, disused factories. Here they slept on the floor and washed in the yard. They were locked in a "closed" camp surrounded by high, barbed wire.

After a while they might move to another, more "open" camp from which they could go out into the community. Once there, officials encouraged them to go out and find work and get together what they could for their future – whatever it might be. It would be in another country, possibly on the other side of the world, because Hong Kong could not possibly keep them permanently. It is already one of the most densely-populated places in the world – although it has never refused anyone first asylum.

Resettlement

Eventually, many of the boat people would be found resettlement places. Many countries responded, the United States, Australia, Canada, Germany and the United Kingdom were among the most generous.

In their host countries the refugees would first spend some time at reception units where families would have private rooms but eat and work together. To make integration into the community as fast and easy as possible, learning the language of the new country would be a priority. Then help and advice in finding

In 1980, over 200,000 people flooded over the Thai-Cambodian border. In the confusion, many families were separated. The UNHCR is specially concerned with the children who cannot find their parents or brothers and sisters. It keeps records of every single person, so if this Cambodian girl saw a familiar face, they would soon be found.

"There is no greater sorrow on earth than the loss of one's native land."

Euripides, 431 B.C.

A place of first asylum. In going to Hong Kong, most of the boat people effectively went to prison, often for many years. Confined in a small place in one of the detention units, its gates firmly locked, they often waited for two years or more to present their case for refugee status. The UN-approved screening process was simply over-burdened. Hong Kong never turned away any asylum seekers but it lacked space and resources to do any more.

them somewhere to live and getting a job would be given. The children, by now many years behind, would start school and get extra help with the language.

Although official policy was to spread refugees around a country, the refugees themselves often moved nearer to each other in groups. Feeling isolated, with language and cultural difficulties – and sometimes hostility from the local population – they felt happier being part of a group and preserving their cultural identity.

More and yet still more...

Between 1975 and 1979 the Vietnamese boat people amounted to over half a million refugees and, in 1979, the UNHCR called a major international conference to try to solve the refugee problem in South East Asia.

As a result, several western governments agreed to take in more of the refugees from the overflowing camps in the various countries of first asylum. China took in a quarter of a million Vietnamese, settling them on state farms and in fishing operations.

One hundred and twenty thousand Vietnamese were flown out of Saigon (Ho Chi Minh City) under the supervision of the UNHCR straight to new homes in the West. This "Orderly Departure Programme", as it was called, was operated by the governments of Vietnam and several western countries. Most of the refugees went to the United States, France, Canada and Australia. These countries then supplied considerable resources to organize the integration of the refugees into their new lives. Given this chance many not only survived, but thrived. They were soon self-sufficient and set up their own businesses.

Worse and worse

But, during the 1980s, the situation in Vietnam worsened. There were now chronic food shortages and people continued to leave in their thousands as they faced starvation at home. They felt they had nothing to lose, whatever the risks of the journey. Under the "Orderly Departure Programme" only so

Intense overcrowding, such as this at the Whitehead detention unit in Hong Kong (above), was gradually relieved by the repatriation of many of the Vietnamese boat people. Left: A new life begins at last as some of the refugees leave the Baton Marong camp for the United States. Their happiness is only spoiled by the sadness of those left behind.

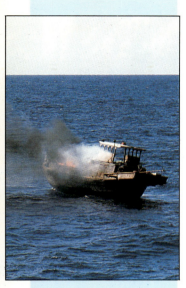

The people on this boat were rescued by a passing cargo boat. Many Vietnamese people set sail in boats like this, knowing they were unseaworthy but preferring to risk the dangers of the South China Sea to persecution or poverty.

"With temporary status, refugees do not need to go through the asylum screening process. These people usually do not want to become citizens of the countries they seek refuge in – all they want is food and shelter until it is safe to go home."

Sylvana Foa, Chief of Public Information for the UNHCR, from "The European", June 1993.

many were allowed to leave each year. Many could wait no longer and set sail.

Most of their vessels were so unseaworthy that their only hope of survival was to be picked up by another ship before they sank. One such "samaritan" vessel was the German ship, *Cap Anamur*. From 1979 to 1982 this converted freighter patrolled the South China Sea to try to help the boat people. On board was a team of doctors and medical volunteers from Germany. They rescued nearly ten thousand boat people.

For about a decade after the boat people first began to arrive, all were granted asylum and refugee status in the countries where they landed. But the welcome got less and less, and in the late 1980s, some countries, such as Malaysia, began to refuse to allow boat people to land. This was obviously disastrous as many had been near starvation when they left Vietnam. It also put ships' captains in a very difficult position when they picked up boat people from sinking boats.

The lucky ones

Those who were "lucky" enough to land, in Hong Kong for instance, faced terrible conditions in the camps. There were now ten of these prison-like detention units. The Hong Kong authorities said they were "doing their best", helped by the UNHCR, but they were fast running out of space. Whole families were squeezed into tiny living areas, with other families right next to them in cage-like containers above, below and on both sides. In some of the camps, there was no running water or electricity. Overcrowding brought disease and tension that led to outbreaks of fighting.

In 1989, the UNHCR called yet another conference to try to solve the problem. It was some fifteen years since the first boat people had left Vietnam. The outcome was a plan under which the countries of the region would grant "first asylum", so that no one would be turned away. UNHCR officials and national immigration officers would then screen and closely question all new arrivals to find out who

fitted in with the UN definition of a refugee. All new asylum seekers would have to prove they were fleeing from persecution and were not economic migrants, people seeking to escape poverty or just to make a better life for themselves.

A permanent solution would be found for those officially recognized as refugees. The economic migrants would be returned to Vietnam – whether they wanted to go or not, under generally accepted international rules.

Forced repatriation

In December 1989, fifty-one boat people, now classed as economic migrants, were put on a plane in Hong Kong and flown back to Vietnam against their will. The plane left Hong Kong in the early hours surrounded by riot police.

There was a world outcry and the plan to send home a further forty thousand Vietnamese was

At Green Island Reception Centre, the space allowed for a whole family unit was about the size of a large bunk bed – with another family on at least two sides. Disused factories and warehouses were used to house many boat people and conditions were harsh with little sanitation and few comforts. Families were kept together but there was no space for privacy. There were plenty of children but no toys, no books, no trees, nowhere to play – little to do but wait.

Each year the UNHCR has to raise the funds necessary to cover its assistance activities for refugees throughout the world. In this way it differs from the majority of the specialized UN agencies, which can rely on a regular budget covered by fixed contributions from each member State.

From *"An instrument of peace," a UNHCR publication.*

temporarily suspended. Boat people in the camps held their own protests, saying they would prefer to stay whatever the conditions there – rather die, than go back. As Thuy, a Vietnamese woman with two young children saw it, "the prisons of Hong Kong are much better than the prisons of Vietnam."

Going back

UNHCR officers began the task of persuading over fifty thousand boat people still in the Hong Kong camps that to return to Vietnam was in their best interest. In accordance with its policy of assisting "returnees", as they are known, the UNHCR offered an allowance to everyone who returned. The European Community also gave aid for development and training projects in Vietnam. To avoid resentment of the returnees by local people, the UNHCR made sure that at least part of such aid went to projects that could be taken advantage of by the whole community.

In Vietnam itself, the UNHCR set up field stations where returnees could bring any problems and UNHCR officials toured remote villages to check on those who could not get to the field stations. The government had agreed to the repatriations and its human rights record had improved; the UNHCR was making sure that no returnees were harassed by officials or persecuted, particularly because they had left Vietnam illegally.

One of the problems was the slowness of the operation. People waited for months in the camps, sometimes up to two years, to have their claims to refugee status heard. About four out of every five claims were rejected. Most were poor farmers and fishermen fleeing from poverty. Even those who agreed to return voluntarily might have to wait months as the Vietnamese government would only take one thousand returnees a month because of the cost of repatriation.

By 1993, there was at last some hope in the long and tragic story of the boat people. The number of people escaping the poverty of Vietnam by boat had dropped to a handful. The economic outlook in

Vietnam was slightly better. There was something worth staying at home for as conditions improved and, for economic migrants, there was the possibility of a future worth going back to. Perversely, it was now those with recognized refugee status who faced the greatest problem, because there were less and less resettlement places available.

Nearly all the challenges and problems that faced the UNHCR after the mid-1970s were highlighted in the story of the Vietnamese boat people. The overwhelming numbers, the years spent in makeshift camps, the doors closing to asylum seekers, the dwindling resettlement places – these were features in many refugee situations, but they were all so graphically illustrated in the plight of the boat people.

Crisis in Afghanistan

Although the Vietnamese exodus may have been the longest sustained flight of refugees in the UNHCR's experience, it did not produce the world's largest

In 1979, Soviet troops entered Afghanistan, which was already experiencing civil unrest. As the Soviets launched their invasion, Afghan people fled to Pakistan and Iran. The UNHCR contributed by providing food, medical units, schooling and employment schemes.

Going home at last...Afghan refugees choose voluntary repatriation, the UNHCR's first solution, after fourteen years in Pakistan. Crafts, tree-planting and income-generating activities were promoted in the camps to ensure the tradition and skills of the Afghan people has not been lost.

refugee population. That was caused by the Soviet invasion of Afghanistan in 1979.

In the ensuing twelve years of civil war, five *million* Afghans fled their country to the shelter of nearby Iran and Pakistan. They were cared for by the UNHCR and, particularly, the government of Iran, at enormous cost. Over the years their poverty increased. They had often fled with flocks of sheep, goats or camels which were soon sold, eaten or became victims of drought or war.

It is hard to envisage suffering on this scale or the chaos caused to the economies of the host countries. How do you cope with an influx of five million people all of whom need food, somewhere to sleep, somewhere to gather firewood, somewhere to work, somewhere to go to school? And the problem did not go away in weeks, months or even a year or two. When the Soviets, at last, withdrew from Afghanistan nine years later, in 1988, there was optimism that the refugees would soon be going

These Mozambican children in Malawi are being given a good start – they are well-fed, have space to play in and are starting school as well. But their world is limited to a refugee camp and even such an excellent host country, such as Malawi, has limited resources. The UNHCR has special plans to help the millions of refugee children around the world. It gives them a chance to go to school and learn about a future in which they are able to take charge of their own lives, back in their homeland or in a new country.

home. But even that optimism proved ill-founded as different factions within Afghanistan struggled for power in the continuing civil war.

Even when all the refugees do eventually return to Afghanistan the young people will have missed years of education. In Iran, for instance, where schools were open to them, many refugee parents were reluctant to send their children because they believe in a different religion. As one elderly refugee commented sadly, as he watched some children playing in the dust, "a whole generation has been lost".

The special problems of children

"Where does rice come from?" a reporter asked three children in a refugee camp in Thailand. "From a truck," they all replied. Their father had been a rice farmer before he fled from Cambodia ten years previously. The children were born in the refugee camp and that was the only world they had ever known. They had never seen rice plants growing in a field.

One of the most difficult problems the UNHCR faces is how to care effectively for refugee children. In many situations, like the civil war in Bosnia, children are often traumatized by the brutality they experience around them – they see their mothers killed in front of their eyes by sniper fire, they attend the funerals of fathers and brothers caught up in the fighting, they lose their toys, they lose their books, they lose contact with television and radio. Even playing in the street becomes a deadly occupation. The happiness and the innocence of childhood is destroyed for ever. The trauma shows on the children's faces and lasts for months and years after they leave, as refugees, to another land.

These are the reasons why the plight of refugee children is of special concern to the UNHCR. It is not enough for a refugee community just to survive people must have a future. It is soul-destroying being trapped in a makeshift camp for years on end and the one hope that adults can cling to is that at least their children will have a future.

The UNHCR gives all the additional help it can to children in the camps, making provision for the extra nutrition that growing children need, taking care of immunization, decent sanitation and education.

Missing school

The UNHCR provides education wherever possible. The schools and training schemes vary a great deal. In some camps they are run by religious leaders; in the Sudan and Pakistan, for example (both countries with large long-term refugee populations), schools have been set up and run by Moslem religious leaders. Their religion can give children a feeling of security; it reminds them of home and links them to other children in the camp and the wider community.

In some camps, schools can teach a wide variety of subjects. In a Cambodian camp in Thailand, for instance, pupils learned reading, grammar and composition, mathematics, science, ethics, geography, art, and music. History is usually

Top: An Afghan Moslem girl learns about her culture in a refugee camp in Pakistan while, in Austria (above), children from different countries all learn the language of their host country.

excluded: it is just too controversial and too hurtful.

When children resettle, the policy is to encourage them to learn about their home country as well as their new country.

Women's rights

Another major problem the UNHCR has to take into account in its management of refugee camps around the world is the role of women. Over two-thirds of the nineteen million refugees in the world today are women and children and the women are often in a particularly vulnerable position.

The UNHCR has been aware for years that women in camps are discriminated against and are in physical danger. They do not have equal access with men to development funds or to take part in projects other than traditional "women's work", such as sewing or cooking. One group of women who ran a successful pig farm were told to sell the pigs and share the profit with the men. But when the possibility of returning home comes at last, the men often get control of everyone's share of the repatriation grant provided by the UNHCR and rarely consult with the women as to how it should be spent. Few women are on the committees that run the camps, but they do most of the work.

Rape and sexual harassment are all too common in the overcrowded and abnormal conditions of camp life. Some women put up with physical abuse, thinking that it is the only way to get food for themselves and their children.

In 1992, the UNHCR held a conference on the problem, FOREFEM, which made everyone realize that women refugees have particular problems. It made several recommendations – to protect women from physical abuse, there should be a female protection officer in every camp, women should be fully involved in development projects and they should carry their own and their family's papers.

Also people in refugee camps often have strong political convictions. They may have fought for the things they believe in. And it is often difficult, in the middle of such strongly-held beliefs, for UNHCR

"Men are free to move. If there is a problem in the camp, they can run. But we women are walking with children and we can't run, we can't move, we can't take any decision to travel as easily as men."
A Somali woman in Ethiopia, from a UNHCR publication.

Opposite: "The refugee problem has a female face" said High Commissioner, Sadako Ogata. The face of this woman shows all the anguish and desolation of refugee women left alone with young children. Women suffer the most in these situations, they are the most vulnerable and they will do anything to protect their children. The UNHCR protects women and the women themselves get together for mutual protection and help.

The first need is to survive. In strife-torn Sudan, ravaged by civil war, starving people with frail skeletal bodies struggle to aid units and refugee camps. If they reach a camp, they may survive but it is increasingly difficult for the UNHCR and other humanitarian agencies to help. Aid is no longer seen as being neutral by the warring groups – they have sometimes used obstruction of the food supply as a weapon against their enemies.

officials to convince refugees that they are not taking sides. They are neutral and they will help both sides and their only objectives are humanitarian.

In the Bosnian civil war in 1993, for example, the UNHCR was accused of assisting Serb policies of "ethnic cleansing" when it rescued Moslem women and children from besieged towns. It was an impossible situation. If it rescued the women and children it was accused of doing the Serbs' work for them; if it left the women and children behind they would be killed by bombardment.

Faced with impossible choices like this, UNHCR officials have to decide where their primary loyalties lie and they always come down on the humanitarian side of saving life and arguing the political niceties later.

In the camps themselves, it is sometimes necessary for the UNHCR to keep different political groups apart. In Cambodian refugee camps near the border in Thailand, for example, the refugees brought their civil war with them. Some 350,000 people were crowded into these camps by the early 1990s and the camps were divided according to the refugees' politics. Some were for non-Communists and some for Communist Khmer Rouge supporters. Armed bands carried out raids across the nearby border and attacked and shelled refugee camps of the rival faction. It does not make for an easy life for the UNHCR staff.

What is the way forward?

When the UNHCR was established in 1951 with a small staff of thirty and a three year mandate, few would have forseen that, by the end of the twentieth century, the problem of refugees would have grown to the scale it has today. We now have a world full of ethnic clashes and a continuing, and seemingly growing, problem of refugees; nineteen million now and who knows how many in the next few years?

Central to the problem facing the UNHCR today is the factor of public opinion. Summed up in a nutshell, most people feel sorry for refugees, but they also don't want them arriving on their doorstep.

If not by foot or by boat, by air

Throughout the 1980s, there was a dramatic increase in the number of asylum seekers arriving by plane. As a result, more and more governments have taken steps to stop asylum seekers entering their countries by air.

Airlines are heavily fined for flying people without entry visas. This means that the airlines are, in a way, made to adopt the role of governments by being forced to decide who can and cannot enter a country.

The UNHCR and other refugee organizations have complained strongly to governments about the whole situation. They feel that, rather than putting up barriers, which may prevent genuine refugees from even reaching their countries, governments should be prepared to give asylum seekers a fair screening.

In 1990 over 150 Kurdish people, desperate to leave Iraq but unable to get on regular

Faced with enforced repatriation to Sri Lanka, Tamil refugees stripped off in front of media cameras at Heathrow Airport, London, England, in 1987. This dramatic plea for help captured the public's attention, bringing the Tamil refugees support as they struggled to gain political asylum. They feared for their lives if they were returned to the civil unrest from which they had fled and no one seemed to want to help them.

flights, finally chartered a plane to fly them to London to request asylum. Sometimes fake passports and visas are used just to enable an asylum seeker to get on a plane. They then hope that immigration officials will, at least, listen to their story. If their application is checked according to internationally-accepted UNHCR procedures they have a chance of obtaining refugee status.

Unfortunately, border authorities do not always listen to their claims. So, when the asylum seekers reach their chosen country, they may be put on a flight out again immediately and shuttled back and forth between countries until they can find one which will listen.

In 1991, four Kurds were flown repeatedly from

A crowd of hungry Ethiopian refugees surge around a shipment of food, gratefully touching the solid reality of the bulging sacks. When the news of the famine reached the West through Bob Geldof's Live Aid in 1987, food and aid flooded into the country. Television and radio soon lose interest in a story – but the UNHCR fights continuously to keep people and governments aware of people in difficulty and urges them to find a safe place for them.

Zurich to Vienna and back again over a period of two weeks. No one would grant even temporary asylum. They were finally taken in at Zurich.

Will no one help?

It is not only at airports that doors are slamming in the faces of asylum seekers. Borders are shutting and laws against them tightening in many countries, particularly in the developed world.

The United States turned back boatloads of Haitians escaping from a military coup, while Italy repatriated thousands of Albanians without giving them a hearing. In Britain, with a backlog of over fifty thousand asylum cases to hear, the law on

"Remember. Refugees are not a threat. They are threatened. They are not a burden on society. They carry society's burden."

From a UNHCR publication.

hearings is to be tightened. Even in Sweden, a country with a long reputation for hospitality, there have been attacks on refugees.

All this threatens the framework of international protection that the UNHCR has painstakingly built up, country by country, around the world over more than forty years. Turning people away at borders endangers the essential principle of first asylum. To the UNHCR, sending people back unheard is unacceptable.

"Nothing against foreigners"

In fact, most countries still want to keep their doors open to refugees, but are concerned about taking in thousands of asylum seekers of whom probably only a small percentage will be granted refugee status. It may take years to hear all the claims which is, in itself, an expensive process. Then, if the application is refused, the person may not want to go back. They probably left to escape poverty and deprivation and they may now have a job and a home.

The host country may allow these economic migrants to stay on but, to prevent this happening in future, may stop new asylum seekers entering the country at all. So, as with the Vietnamese boat people, large numbers of economic migrants block up the system for those who are genuinely fleeing from persecution.

Countries also reduce the number of resettlement places offered to refugees to "balance" the total number they take in. In fact, most refugees are in the developing world and they form only a very small part of the prosperous countries' populations. The numbers knocking at the doors of the industrialized world are still only a tiny minority but, if they are of different ethnic and cultural origins, they may also face opposition because of their race.

Telling the truth

There is often genuine sympathy and generous charitable giving when refugees are seen on television and in newspapers escaping from some

"The challenges in the world today in terms of refugees, displaced or repatriating populations, appear arduous as ever and can only be resolved with a constant common effort on the part of the international community, which the High Commissioner is called upon to coordinate."

From "An instrument of peace", a UNHCR publication.

Opposite: Asylum seekers trying to fill their time as they wait to hear whether they will be granted refugee status in Athens, Greece. The problem for the UNHCR is not finding money to help refugees but finding a country that will take them. People are happy to give money but do not want to live next to "foreigners" – the UNHCR has a long, hard battle against this attitude.

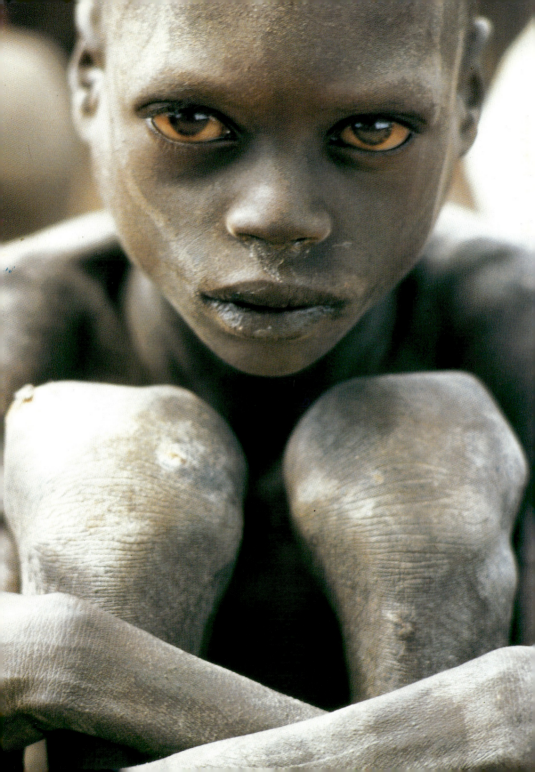

desperate situation. But people may not feel the same sympathy if those seeking asylum come to live in the same street as them.

People can feel threatened by the different customs and beliefs of others. They fear they will be swamped by huge numbers and lose their own way of life.

The media does not always help. It can play on people's fears, whipping up panic to make a sensational story to sell newspapers. To tell the facts, to explain who asylum seekers are and why they are here, is far more difficult and not necessarily "newsworthy".

The UNHCR, as an essential part of its task of protecting refugees and creating a climate of safety and welcome for them, has to be concerned with public attitudes. There is a special information section at the Geneva headquarters with a director who speaks for the High Commissioner and is in close touch with the world's media.

So the UNHCR encourages news reporters with

This page and opposite: Supplies arrive, food is distributed, a hungry child waits patiently. He is alive but can his steady gaze see a real future?

A child and his mother, forced to leave their whole life behind, their family torn apart. They are leaving Sarajevo in Bosnia, driven out by war and ethnic cleansing. Their faces tell it all. They are refugees.

"Do they think we like being refugees, that we have left our homes willingly?"

Mufida Hadzlhasanovic,
a Bosnian refugee,
from "The European", June 1993.

---

cameras to visit areas with large refugee populations and to talk to the refugees and take pictures of their appalling circumstances. It sometimes does this despite opposition by local authorities who don't want the media involved. Only in this way can the real truth come out.

Putting together the often harrowing stories may help people to understand that refugees have been forced to leave their country. They can identify with the refugees' loss and fears as individual human beings and not think of them as a faceless, threatening mass. They may then be motivated to accept and help them and to realize that refugees are victims, but also they are resourceful people. There is nothing that refugees would rather do than go home – if only they could.

Important Dates

1921	The League of Nations appoints Fridtjof Nansen as the first High Commissioner for Refugees.
1951	Jan 1: The Office of the United Nations High Commissioner for Refugees (UNHCR), created by the UN General Assembly, begins operations. July 28: The UN Convention relating to the status of refugees is adopted.
1953	The UN General Assembly reviews the need to prolong the UNHCR's three-year mandate. The mandate is renewed and has been every five years since then.
1954	The UNHCR is awarded the Nobel Prize for Peace.
1959	World Refugee Year is celebrated, drawing public attention to the problems of refugees and raising funds to help them.
1967	Jan 31: The Protocol to the 1951 Convention on refugees is adopted in New York, United States. This extends the time limit of the Convention to people who were made refugees after 1951.
1969	Sept: A convention is adopted by the Organization of African Unity (OAU) that extends the definition of refugees in Africa to explicitly include people who have fled their countries because of conflict and disorder as well as persecution.
1971	The UNHCR deals with its first refugee emergency involving millions of people, when some ten million Bengalis flee from East Pakistan to India.
1975	The first boat people sail from Vietnam in an exodus that is to continue for seventeen years, the longest sustained flight in the history of the UNHCR.
1979	Afghan refugees begin to flee in startling numbers to Pakistan and Iran, making it the largest scale crisis with which the UNHCR has had to deal so far. The UNHCR calls for a major international conference to deal with the refugee problems in South East Asia.
1981	The UNHCR is awarded the Nobel Prize for Peace for a second time.
1989	An International Conference on South East Asia adopts a Comprehensive Plan of Action (CPA) to try to provide solutions to the boat people crisis and other issues in the region.
1991	The exodus of the Kurds from Iraq and the operation to return them home safely are perhaps the fastest movements to have occurred on such a scale in refugee history.
1992	The UNHCR becomes increasingly involved in the civil war in former Yugoslavia. The war creates the largest refugee crisis in Europe since World War II and new problems for the UNHCR as it works constantly in the war zone. Mrs. Sadako Ogata, elected United Nations High Commissioner for Refugees in 1991, initiates a "Year of Repatriation". A UNHCR conference, FOREFEM, is held concerning the particular problems facing women refugees.
1993	By the end of the year, the total number of refugees rises to more than nineteen million. Over the previous decade the total had grown by an average of nearly one million each year.

Glossary

Allied troops: In this instance, the military personnel representing twenty-eight countries, including the United Kingdom and the United States of America, against Iraq during the Gulf War in 1991.

Artillery: Heavy firearms used in warfare.

Asylum: A place of safety, a refuge. International law states that the individual has the right to seek sanctuary in another country, if that individual is in danger in the country of origin.

Asylum seeker: A person who leaves his or her home country and is seeking *refugee* status in another country. Not all asylum seekers are recognized as genuine refugees.

Civil war: War between different groups of people in the same country.

Colony: A country that is conquered and ruled by another, usually from a great distance. The invading country establishes settlements, with the settlers remaining subjects of the invading country.

Communism: A form of governing based on the economic ideas of Karl Marx and, later, Vladimir Lenin. The central belief is that each person should work according to their ability and receive according to their need. Karl Marx supported the idea of equal distribution of wealth, where capitalism is replaced by a working class government for a classless society.

Displaced person: Originally a term referring to the deportation of a civilian from a German-occupied country to work in Germany during World War II, after which he or she became homeless. The term is now used to describe anyone forced to leave their home, and includes *refugees* (people forced to leave their homes *and* their countries).

Economic migrant: A person who leaves his or her country in search of a better standard of living in another country.

Ethnic: An ethnic group is a group of people who think of themselves as being of the same kind; they may share a variety of features, such as race, culture, nationality, and religion.

Ethnic cleansing: The name given to the practice in the *civil war* in former Yugoslavia of creating so-called "ethnically pure" areas by forcibly relocating or murdering members of all other groups.

Exodus: The departure of many people at the same time, often suddenly.

Fugitive: Someone who is fleeing, usually from arrest or pursuit.

Host country: The country to which *asylum seekers* have fled and, having been granted *refugee* status, may later be allowed to live in permanently.

Guerrilla: A person fighting in an unofficial and independent unit against the recognized or ruling forces.

Humanitarian: Concern for the well-being of humankind.

Immigrant: A person who comes into a country to settle from a different country.

Immigration: The movement of people into a country to work and live; laws relating to *refugees* are often part of immigration laws and *asylum seekers* are interviewed by immigration officials.

Integration: A policy to absorb changes, in this instance the helping of incoming *refugees* to settle in the established community.

Khmer Rouge: A Communist *guerrilla* organization in Cambodia that has been active since the 1960s. The Khmer Rouge took control between 1975-1979, exercising a severe regime.

League of Nations: An international organization formed in 1919 in order to try to resolve international disputes through discussion. The organization was made up from states around the world, but the decision of the United States not to join limited the power of the organization, which broke up in the mid-1940s. It was succeeded by the formation of the *United Nations* in 1945.

Mandate: When authority is given to a body or organization to carry out specific policies.

Nazi: A member of the National Socialist German Workers' Party, that came to power in 1933 under the dictatorship of Adolf Hitler.

Non-governmental organization (NGO): A voluntary organization, not run by government; the UNHCR relies on the help of about two hundred NGOs as partners in implementing its policies around the world.

Persecution: Ill-treatment, such as being subjected to

continual harassment, even tortured or threatened with death, due to race, religion or political beliefs.
Refugee: Someone who is fleeing his or her own country, driven out by a well-founded fear of *persecution* or because of the dangers of war or *civil war*.
Repatriation: The act of someone returning to his or her home country. This can be an enforced policy (when it is known as re-foulement) or people can repatriate voluntarily, often with the help of the UNHCR.
Sanctuary: A place where a *fugitive* can stay in safety.
Trauma: An emotional shock that can have a long-lasting effect.
United Nations (UN): An international organization of countries to maintain world peace and security and to promote cultural, social and economic cooperation. It was established in 1945 as a successor to the *League of Nations* and has more than 150 members. Its headquarters are in New York.
UN Refugee Convention, 1951: The most important legal agreement concerned with *refugees;* it provides a definition of the term *"refugee"* and sets out minimum standards for their treatment.
World Health Organization (WHO): WHO was established in 1948 as an agency of the *United Nations.* Its aim is to promote health and to control, and hopefully prevent, the spread of disease.

Further Information

If you would like to find out more information about the work of the UNHCR, contact the organization in your country. Address any of your enquiries to the Public Information Section.

UNHCR Regional Office for Australia, New Zealand and the South Pacific
9 Terrigal Crescent O'Malley
Canberra A.C.T. 2606
Australia

UNHCR Branch Office in Canada
280 Albert Street
Suite 401
Ottawa
Ontario KIP 5G8
Canada

UNHCR Branch Office for the United Kingdom and Ireland
7 Westminster Palace Gardens
Artillery Row
London SW1P 1RL
United Kingdom

UNHCR Branch Office for the United States
1718 Connecticut Avenue N.W.
2nd Floor
Washington D.C. 20009
U.S.A.

UNHCR Headquarters
Case Postale 2500
CH-1211 Genève 2 Dépot
Switzerland

Index

Afghanistan 45
  civil war in 47-48
Africa
  civil war in 32-33

"Blue Routes" 11
Boat people 35-45
  forced repatriation of 43-44
  plan to help 42-43

Civil war
  in Afghanistan 47-48
  in Africa 32-33
  in East Pakistan 34-35
  in Ethiopia 21
  in former Yugoslavia 11-15, 52
Communism **62**
  in Eastern Europe 29
  Khmer Rouge and 37, 52, **62**

East Pakistan
  crisis in 34-35
Economic migrants 24, 43, 57
  definition of 22
El Salvador 25
Ethiopia
  civil war in 21
  famine in 21
Ethnic cleansing 12, 52, **62**

FOREFEM 51

Gulf War 7, 9
  "Blue Routes" 11

Hong Kong 42, 44
  "closed" and "open" camps 39
  conditions in 42

Immigration 24, **62**
Integration
  policy of 23, 39, **62**
International Refugee Year 31
Iraq
  and the Gulf War 6-8
  Kurds flee from 5-11, 53-54, 54-55

Khmer Rouge 37, 52, **62**
Kurds 5-11, 22, 53-54, 54-55

League of Nations 16, **62**

Nansen, Fridtjof 16

Nansen passport 16

"Orderly Departure Programme" 40

Refugees
  African 21, 32-33, 35
  camps 7, 11, 20, 28, 35, 39
  case histories of 14-15, 20, 25, 27, 30
  Chinese 32
  definition of 19, 22, **62**
  European 11-15, 28-29
  integration policy for 23, 39, **62**
  Kurdish 5-11, 22, 53, 54
  media interest in 11, 14, 57-60
  numbers of 7, 12, 22, 26, 28, 29, 31, 32, 33, 34, 40, 47, 51, 52
  Pakistani 34-35
  persecution of 5-11, 12-15, 16, 18, 20, 21, 25, 27, 29, 30, 35, 37
  plight of, and help for children 40, 48-51
  problems facing 17-18, 23-24, 39-40, 42, 52-60
  problems facing women 51
  reception units for 39
  repatriation of 22, 43, 62
  resettlement of 23, 28, 31, 35, 39, 40, 44
  "returnees" scheme for 44
  right of asylum for 14-15
  Vietnamese 35-45, 57
    forced repatriation of 43-44
    plan to help 42-43

United Nations (UN) 16, **62**
  and "Blue Routes" 11
  and the Gulf War 7, 9
  and the setting up of UNHCR 17
  and Convention relating to the status of refugees (1951) 19, 24
    and 1967 Protocol 19
UN Convention relating to the status of refugees (1951) 19, 24
United Nations High Commissioner for Refugees (UNHCR)
  and case histories of refugees 14-15, 20, 25, 27, 30
  difficulties facing 11, 17-18, 45, 52-60
  first High Commissioner of 16
  and FOREFEM conference 51
  headquarters of 7, 9, 26
  and International Refugee Year 31
  mandate for 17, 18, 32
  preparation by 7, 9, 11
    and provision for basic needs of refugees 48-51
  resources of 11, 26
  role of 7, 12-14, 18-19, 22-23, 26, 33, 47, 49
  and schemes to help refugees
    agricultural settlements 34
    educational 49-51
    "Orderly Departure Programme" 40
    repatriation 22, 43, **62**
    resettlement 23, 28, 31, 35, 40, 44
    returnees 44
    screening of refugees 42-43
  setting up of 17, 52
  staff of 26-28
  support from other organizations 28
  and work with governments 24, 26, 33

Vietnam
  plight of boat people 35-45, 57

War atrocities 12, 14-15, 18, 21, 25, 27, 30
World Health Organization (WHO) 28, **63**
World War II 12, 16, 28, 32

Yugoslavia, former state of
  civil war in 11-15
  ethnic cleansing in 12, 52

Sexsmith Secondary School Library